**ANIMAL FAMILIES**

DOLPHINS
LIFE IN THE POD

Willow Clark

PowerKiDS press™

New York

Published in 2011 by The Rosen Publishing Group, Inc.
29 East 21st Street, New York, NY 10010

First Edition

Editor: Jennifer Way
Book Design: Julio Gil

Photo Credits: Cover, pp. 4–5, 9, 15 (right), 19, 21, 23, 24 (top left, bottom) iStockphoto/Thinkstock; back cover © www.iStockphoto.com/Alexey Bannykh; pp. 7, 11 (top), 13, 24 (top right) Comstock/ Thinkstock; pp. 11 (bottom), 14–15 (main, left) Shutterstock.com; p. 17 David J. Slater/Getty Images.

Library of Congress Cataloging-in-Publication Data

Clark, Willow.
  Dolphins : life in the pod / by Willow Clark. — 1st ed.
      p. cm. — (Animal families)
  Includes bibliographical references and index.
  ISBN 978-1-4488-2512-7 (library binding) — ISBN 978-1-4488-2610-0 (pbk.) —
ISBN 978-1-4488-2611-7 (6-pack)
  1. Dolphins—Juvenile literature. 2. Familial behavior in animals—Juvenile literature. I. Title.
  QL737.C432C55 2011
  599.53—dc22
                                            2010019399

Manufactured in the United States of America

CPSIA Compliance Information: Batch #WW11PK: For Further Information contact Rosen Publishing, New York, New York at 1-800-237-9932

CONTENTS

Dolphins live in groups, called **pods**.

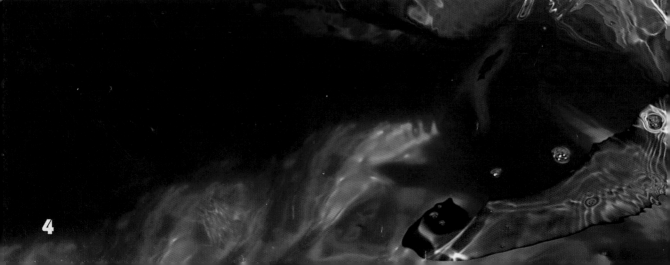

A pod can have any number of dolphins. Some pods have hundreds of dolphins.

Dolphins breathe air through **blowholes** at the tops of their heads.

Blowhole

Spotted dolphins and spinner dolphins are two kinds of dolphins.

Spotted Dolphin

Spinner Dolphin

11

Dolphins make sounds to talk to other dolphins.

The pod works together to hunt for food. Dolphins eat fish, squid, and shrimp.

Shrimp

Fish

When a dolphin finds fish to eat, it makes sounds to tell the rest of the pod.

The pod works together when a member is hurt. The pod helps it come up for air.

Baby dolphins are called **calves**. The mother dolphin helps her calf learn to swim.

Calves stay with their mothers when they are young.

Words to Know

blowhole

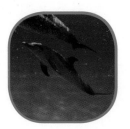

calf

pod

Index

Web Sites

Due to the changing nature of Internet links, PowerKids Press has developed an online list of Web sites related to the subject of this book. This site is updated regularly. Please use this link to access the list:
www.powerkidslinks.com/afam/dolphin/